Weather in Spring

BY M. J. YORK

Published by The Child's World®
1980 Lookout Drive • Mankato, MN 56003-1705
800-599-READ • www.childsworld.com

Photographs ©: iStockphoto, cover, 1, 10, 19; Maxim
Petrichuk/Shutterstock Images, 5; Shutterstock Images, 6,
13, 20–21; Creative Travel Projects/Shutterstock Images,
8–9; T. M. McCarthy/Shutterstock Images, 14; Ivan
Kuzmin/Shutterstock Images, 16–17

Design Element: Shutterstock Images

ISBN 9781503816589
LCCN 2016945622

Printed in the United States of America
PA02324

ABOUT THE AUTHOR

M. J. York is a writer and editor
from Minnesota. She enjoys spring
rains and planting her garden.

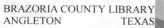
Contents

Warmer Weather

It is spring. The snow melts.

5

Spring comes after the cold winter. **Temperatures** warm up.

The days grow longer. The sun rises earlier. It sets later.

It rains in spring.

Sometimes it storms.

Spring Changes

Plants grow again.

Flowers **bloom**.

Animals eat the new plants. Many animals have babies.

Some birds flew south for the winter. It was warmer there. Now they come back.

Spring Clothes

We feel it warm up in spring. We wear lighter **layers**. We wear spring jackets.

Spring keeps getting warmer. Soon summer will be here!

21

Rainbow-in-the-Clouds Craft

Rainbows can appear after a spring rain. Make your own rainbow!

Supplies:

white paper plate	cotton balls
box of crayons	glue

Instructions:

1. Use your crayons to color a rainbow on the top half of the plate. Start with red on the outside. Follow with a row of orange, yellow, green, blue, and then purple.

2. Spread glue on the bottom of half of the plate.

3. Place cotton balls on the glue to make clouds!

Glossary

bloom — (BLOOM) To bloom means to produce flowers. Plants bloom in spring.

layers — (LAY-urz) Layers are coatings of something. We wear lighter layers in spring when it warms up.

temperatures — (TEM-pur-uh-churz) Temperatures are how warm or cold things are. The temperatures in spring get warmer and warmer.

To Learn More

Books

Aloian, Molly. *How Do We Know It Is Spring?* New York, NY: Crabtree Publishing Company, 2013.

Amoroso, Cynthia, and Robert B. Noyed. *Spring.* Mankato, MN: The Child's World, 2014.

Web Sites

Visit our Web site for links about spring weather: **childsworld.com/links**

Note to Parents, Teachers, and Librarians: We routinely verify our Web links to make sure they are safe and active sites. So encourage your readers to check them out!

Index